HOLLYWOOD PORTRAITS

HOLLYWOOD PORTRAITS
CLASSIC SCENE STILLS 1939-1951
MARK VIEIRA

MALLARD
PRESS

Dedication: To my Mother, Father, Sister Plum and 'Tookie.'

Special thanks to Harrison Sheppard, David Chierichetti, Harvey Stewart, and David Noh.

Copyright © 1989 by Brompton Books Corp

First published in the United States of America in 1989 by The Mallard Press
Mallard Press and its accompanying design and logo are trademarks of BDD Promotional Book Company, Inc.

ISBN 0-792-45076-0

Printed in Italy

Page 1: A portrait of starlet Ava Gardner by Eric Carpenter, circa 1944.

Pages 2–3: Anne Shirley, Miles Mander, Claire Trevor and Dick Powell in a scene from Edward Dmytryk's 1944 RKO production **Murder My Sweet**.

These pages: Cary Grant and Joan Fontaine in **Suspicion**.

INTRODUCTION

In my 1988 book *Hollywood Portraits*, I conducted a tour through my file cabinet, the contents of which were still photographs made to promote motion pictures of the 1930s. The tour ended at the close of that decade; my collection does not. With *Hollywood Portraits II*, I am returning to the last year of that decade and continuing my tour.

Nineteen thirty-nine was a watershed year if ever there was one. Fashion, culture, economics and politics all felt the chill winds of change. Hollywood felt them too. As if expecting to be judged by posterity, the studios produced a portfolio of classic motion pictures. This collective portfolio included **Stagecoach**, **The Hunchback of Notre Dame**, **Gunga Din**, **Midnight**, **Dark Victory**, **Mr Smith Goes To Washington**, **Destry Rides Again**, **The Wizard Of Oz**, **Ninotchka**, **The Women** and of course, **Gone With The Wind**.

As a neophyte film buff growing up in Oakland, I learned to hold this year in awe. I also learned to regard it as the point beyond which I need not venture. What few films from the 1940s I'd seen on television left that impression intact.

How could Hollywood improve on perfection? The 1930s, the Golden Era of Glamour, had ended and in its place bloomed a time of zoot suits, pompadours, jitterbugs—and movies that contained those unlovely images. If the *TV Guide* listed an upcoming 'Late Show' as having been made after 1939, I didn't want to see it.

Then on a fateful Friday night in my senior year of high school, the local television station failed to broadcast a film I'd been planning to watch: a 1932 melodrama called **The Devil And The Deep**. In its place the station broadcast the 1949 fantasy **Portrait Of Jennie**, which began without even the credit sequence I'd learned to scan for copyright date. The credits, of course, would have given me a chance to escape the room with an obligatory 'Ugh! The Forties!' but since there were no credits, I was caught unaware—and immediately entranced. My tastes were soon broadened, and of course this beautifully crafted film was the work of artists whose 1930s oeuvre was already dear to my heart.

I began to look at 1940s Hollywood with a less jaundiced eye, and investigated more films of the period. I came to realize that the luster I'd associated with the 1930s actually reached its apex in the late 1940s. The technical virtuosity of films like **The Locket** and **The Razor's Edge** were undeniable, as was also the subtlety of their themes.

The films of the 1940s were sophisticated in a way I hadn't yet encountered (or understood), because they came from a time when the harsh realities of wartime life could not be escaped as readily as the woes of the Depression had been. The horrors of war had to be dealt with, as well as political and psychological issues. The films of the 1940s emerged as products of a mature time, and as works of a matured art form—both in form and content. The gauzy, brash beauty of the early 'Talkies' had evolved into the self-assured Expressionism of 'the Movies.'

This process of evolution (and time itself) turned several of my personally most revered countenances into *démodé* dinosaurs. Their absence from 1940s movie screens had been one reason for my initial resistance. Greta Garbo, for instance, had made a token effort to change with the times, but after being accorded a lukewarm reception, decided that the effort was not worthwhile. Marlene Dietrich, on the other hand, thought otherwise and made a successful transition.

The remaking and unmaking of these stars has left a legacy of images as fascinating as those from the early 1930s. These images, as well as those of the 'new stars' of the 1940s, comprise my movie photo collection. I've spent 15 years amassing it, and it now fills a legal size file cabinet. My collection is a modest one compared to collections of other private 'still' collectors, but I feel that it has grown large enough to be of some interest to you.

In sharing it with you, I show you a collection of images that is not intended to be a comprehensive representation of 1940s Hollywood. When I purchased the photographic prints you see on these pages—and I purchased them mostly in the Los Angeles

Left: Mr Mark Alan Vieira

Facing page: Marlene Dietrich adapted and thrived in comic vehicles like George Marshall's **Destry Rides Again**, which was a 1939 Universal production.

area—it was because I wanted a sampling of the skillfully created images from films that I had viewed, re-viewed and loved.

Portrait Of Jennie is not *only* a magical experience in itself. It also occasioned the creation of magical images—images that can stand on their own. They are as alluring, entrancing and powerful as the film they were meant to publicize.

These images—whether 'scene stills,' 'behind-the-scene stills' or 'portrait art'—are also inspiring. I've certainly found them so. They inspired me to make student films, to emulate their craftsmanship and ultimately to embark on a career as a portrait photographer. As you may suspect, my portrait work is executed 'in the classic Hollywood mode.'

It was therefore the fulfillment of a long-felt desire that, when having studied the work of RKO portraitist Ernest A Bachrach, I was granted a portrait session by one of his loveliest subjects, Jane Greer (*facing page*).

Her performance in Jacques Tourneur's classic **Out Of The Past** is for me one of the high-water marks of *film noir* history, and having exalted her to that status, I was doubly gratified to hear her compare my work to that of Mr Bachrach. As you'll see in the pages devoted to **Out Of The Past**, the magic is as much hers as his—but this is the mystique of Hollywood itself. Talent, dedication and skill—both in front of the camera and behind it—combine images and stories and *more* images that you see, and remember, and want to see again.

If you haven't seen the films themselves, then I hope that the images I'm presenting to you will make you want to see the films from which they derive. If you've already seen them, I hope that these images will affect you as they do me; in other words, I hope you enjoy them!

Mark Alan Vieira

Mark A Vieira, San Francisco
25 April 1988

Above: The principals of Victor Fleming's **The Wizard Of Oz** move apprehensively through the Emerald Forest and into the future. Most of the incredible revenues earned by this MGM film would indeed come from the future (television) and not from 1939 audiences, who apparently believed disdainful critics. Unfortunately, those revenues would never find their way to Jack Haley, Judy Garland or Ray Bolger, who are shown here.

MGM's 1939 production of **The Women** was an oddity for its time — or any time — because its cast was composed solely of women. Clare Booth Luce's 1936 play had been purchased as a potential vehicle for Jean Harlow, but Miss Harlow had died by the time of its production. Anita Loos and Jane Murfin tailored the script to Legion of Decency standards while also adding their characteristic bite. The result, as directed by George Cukor, the ultimate women's director, has become an enduring classic and perhaps his most enjoyable film, if only because he so much enjoyed working with this temperamental ensemble.

Above, left to right: Front row, Norma Shearer, Rosalind Russell, George Cukor, producer Hunt Stromberg, and Paulette Goddard; back row, Joan Crawford, Joan Fontaine, Mary Boland, Phyllis Povah, and Florence Nash.

Right: Inventive publicity stills like this one made sure that every possible angle of a production was covered — and was therefore newsworthy. This one, though, brings to mind two incidents that never made it to print in 1939. The first incident took place when Rosalind Russell packed up her makeup kit and went on strike for equal billing with Shearer and Crawford.

Facing page: The second incident was incited by Joan Crawford's ever-present knitting needles, which she clicked so loudly during Norma Shearer's rehearsal that Norma left the set in a huff. This portrait evokes the following excerpt from Loos/Murfin's screenplay:

   Mary Haines: You're even more typical than I dared hope.
   Crystal: Well, honey, that goes double!
   The hilarious finale of the film brought the entire cast together. Another excerpt from the screenplay . . .
   Crystal: Well, girls . . . looks like it's back to the perfume counter for me. And by the way, there's a name for you ladies. But it isn't used in high society — outside of a kennel.

Above: George Cukor tells Mary Boland how to say this line, 'Get me a bromide — and put some gin in it!'

Facing page: Never reluctant to mug, Rosalind Russell stole the show from her more restrained co-stars, all of whom had incidentally auditioned for the role of Scarlett O'Hara. Paulette Goddard got her role in **The Women** because George Cukor directed her **Gone With The Wind** screen test and liked her.

Above: John Kobal's milestone book *The Art of the Great Holly-wood Portrait Photographers* describes the Laszlo Willinger sitting that produced this quirky trio's portraits. There were seemingly endless cancellations, rescheduling, delays and tardiness; Norma pulled rank when she felt like pulling hair, and Rosalind Russell was summarily dismissed from the set — it was all in a day's work at Metro. This photo was finally made on 22 May 1939. Thirty years later, Joan Crawford was known to remark: 'Well, *I* got the gold sequin dress.'

Facing page: Here is an unidentified model in one of the fashion layout shots that comprise at least a third of the 400 key set stills from **The Women**; photo by Carpenter, gown by Adrian.

Facing page: Fred Astaire and Rita Hayworth in the 1942 Columbia motion picture **You Were Never Lovelier**, which also featured Xavier Cugat and his orchestra.

Above: The most famous dancing duo of the 1940s, Fred Astaire and Ginger Rogers. Miss Rogers is here pictured in a still from the Paramount picture, **Sitting Pretty**, in which she starred with Jack Oakie, Jack Haley and Thelma Todd.

Above: A scene still from the legendary 1941 Warner Brothers production, **The Maltese Falcon**, which was based on the classic detective story by Dashiell Hammett. Humphrey Bogart, Peter Lorre, Mary Astor and Sydney Greenstreet gather around the object of their desire.

Above: Born Laslo Lowenstein in Hungary in 1904, Peter Lorre received stage training in Vienna and made his debut in Zurich. After stage experience in Switzerland, Austria and Germany, plus supporting roles in German films, he starred in Fritz Lang's 1931 melodrama, **M** —in which his brilliant portrayal of a psychopathic murderer on the run from the police established him as an actor.

He exiled himself from Germany when the Nazis came to power in 1933—and in 1935, he settled in Hollywood. His early roles in America included that of Raskolnikov in Josef von Sternberg's 1935 film adaptation of Dostoevsky's **Crime and Punishment**; and the oriental detective Mr Moto in a low-budget film series of the late 1930s.

Perhaps his most well-known portrayals, however, were in Warner Brothers dramas of the 1940s, which included his portrayal of Sydney Greenstreet's sidekick in **The Maltese Falcon**, and roles in **The Mask of Dimitrios**, **The Verdict** and **Casablanca**, where he once again starred with Humphrey Bogart. Mr Lorre's portrayals of borderline, dispossessed characters made his very mannerisms the popular hallmark of all that is eerie—and dangerous.

Above: Vivien Leigh and Clark Gable as Scarlett O'Hara and Rhett Butler in a scene still from **Gone With the Wind** (1939). The making of this Selznick International Pictures epic was extremely stressful, and involved, among other things, a change of directors — from George Cukor to Victor Fleming. **Gone with the Wind** was released through MGM.

Facing page: The usually imperturbable Clark Gable was also affected by the ordeal of making **Gone With The Wind**. Clarence Bull's sympathetic portrait manner could not allay or disguise Gable's unease in this June 1939 portrait.

Above: Clark Gable awaits a cue to drive Melanie and baby (offscene) through the night. *Below:* Vivien Leigh in a scene still showing Ernie Haller's lighting effects.

Facing page: In retrospect, the Academy Award given to Vivien Leigh was but the beginning of a lifetime of laurels occasioned by her performance in **Gone With the Wind**.

Above: The still camera caught this famous foursome during a rehearsal on **The Wizard Of Oz** set. They are, from left to right, Ray Bolger as the Scarecrow, Jack Haley as the Tin Man, Judy Garland (of course!) as Dorothy and Bert Lahr as the Cowardly Lion.

Facing page: Second only to the Crawford-Shearer feud was that of Miriam Hopkins and Bette Davis. It was arbitrated by another gifted 'woman's director,' Edmund Goulding, for **The Old Maid**, produced in 1939 at Warner Brothers. This portrait was made by Bert Six.

Below: Greta Garbo and Bela Lugosi had one scene together in Ernst Lubitsch's 1939 MGM production, **Ninotchka**. This represented the first comedy role for either of them.

Above: Charles Laughton painted a fresh character portrait of Victor Hugo's pathetic Quasimodo—in William Dieterle's **The Hunchback Of Notre Dame**, which was produced in 1939 at RKO.

Facing page: John Ford's 1939 United Artists production, **Stagecoach**, made John Wayne a star, lifting both him and Claire Trevor out of the 'B movie' assembly line.

Above: Humphrey Bogart was on the verge of stardom when this portrait was made by George Hurrell.

Above: Errol Flynn's stardom lasted into the 1940s, but he then had to 'move over' for Bogart.

Above: 'Mrs Clark Gable:' This portrait shows Carole Lombard in her favorite role . . . as the wife of Clark Gable. She is here shown in one of the barns on their Encino ranch.

Facing page: Carole Lombard appeared to be bound for even greater stardom in the 1940s, but her ascent was cut short by a plane crash following a war bond tour. This scene is from Garson Kanin's **They Knew What They Wanted**, produced in 1940 at RKO.

Above: A Lombard portrait, made at the Selznick studio by Ted Allan—before he took his imaginative portrait style to the CBS radio network.

Facing page: Laszlo Willinger was another portraitist who chose to leave the Hollywood studio environment in order to concentrate on commercial photography. Before he did, though, he spent seven years making movie industry icons of all the MGM stars who sat for him—including Vivien Leigh, here shown in a portrait from Mervyn LeRoy's **Waterloo Bridge**, which was produced in 1940 at MGM.

Above: The most popular portrait photographer operating a gallery outside studio walls was John Engstead. Even Marlene Dietrich entrusted him with her carefully engineered image—but even at that, her mentor, Josef von Sternberg, always had to come along. John deferred to Sternberg's visual genius, and the result was this portrait for Tay Garnett's 1940 Universal production, **Seven Sinners**.

Facing page: The old guard at the studio was represented by the dignified Clarence Sinclair Bull, who continued as head of MGM's gallery into the 1940s. He made this portrait of Judy Garland just after **The Wizard Of Oz**.

Above: Susan Hayward was an ubiquitous starlet until she played a provocative small-town hoyden in Paramount's 1941 **Among the Living**, directed by Stuart Heisler.

Facing page: Another adaptation was John Cromwell's film of Joseph Conrad's **Victory**. The producers insisted on a happy ending, but Fredric March (shown here) gave his usual incisive performance in this 1940 Paramount production.

Pages 38–39: William Wyler's **The Letter**, produced in 1940 at Warner Brothers, gave Bette Davis a superb vehicle for her fiery talents, and once again presented her as a Somerset Maugham villainess.

Above: A Bert Six portrait, and, from Howard Koch's screenplay —
Leslie: Every time I met him I'd hate myself. And yet I lived for the moment when I'd see him again. It was horrible. There was never an hour when I was at peace, when I wasn't reproaching myself. I was like a person who is sick with some loathsome disease and doesn't want to get well. Even my agony was a kind of joy. . . .

Facing page: Another Bert Six portrait of Bette Davis from **The Letter**.

Above: Joan Crawford, fresh from her success as a husband-snatching witch in **The Women**, took her cue from Mesdemoiselles Tierney, Davis et al and essayed an unglamorous, gutsy role—sans makeup—in Frank Borzage's **Strange Cargo**. This Willinger portrait shows her with her co-star for this 1940 MGM production, Clark Gable.

Facing page: Marlene Dietrich, along with Joan Crawford, Fred Astaire and Katharine Hepburn, had been labeled 'box-office poison' in a 1938 exhibitors' poll. Marlene saved her plummeting career by spoofing the exotic glamour created for her by Josef von Sternberg; this new slant lasted through the 1940s and several studios. Universal was the unlikely setting for this makeover, and George Marshall's **Destry Rides Again**, the vehicle. This Ray Jones portrait was made to publicize it—but with the assistance of *maestro* Sternberg.

Above: Norma Shearer had also scored a success in **The Women**. Not to be outdone by Joan Crawford, she too chose a topical subject for her first film of the 1940s — Nazi concentration camps. In Mervyn LeRoy's **Escape**, Norma matched wits (and profiles) with a sleekly menacing Nazi. The Nazi was played by the man who must have originated the role, Conrad Veidt. The following is an excerpt from the Arch Oboler-Marguerite Roberts screenplay.

Kurt: That stupid doctor you sent me to warned me against two things. One was violent exercise like skiing. The other was violent quarrels. At the present I prefer skiing. The doctor is an idiot and so are you, my dear, but as usual, I forgive you.

Facing page: Katharine Hepburn revived her career with a hit play and then with a self-produced hit movie adapted from it. George Cukor's **The Philadelphia Story**, produced in 1940 at MGM, re-established Hepburn as a unique screen presence and gave her the clout to bargain for her next career phase: a teaming with Spencer Tracy. This portrait was made by Clarence Sinclair Bull.

Pages 46–47: A Bull portrait of Tracy and Hepburn for George Stevens' **The Woman Of The Year**, which was an MGM production in 1942.

Above: A Willinger portrait of Joan Crawford and Fredric March in George Cukor's **Susan and God**, produced in 1940 at MGM. This was one of the roles Miss Crawford fought for in a never-ending effort to expand her range. This role presented audiences with a self-indulgent society woman who espouses a moral rearmament-like philosophy—ironically, at the expense of her own marriage.

Facing page: As one MGM team was born, another was fading. Produced in 1940, Robert Z Leonard's **New Moon** was the fifth pairing of Jeanette MacDonald and Nelson Eddy; it lacked their usual spark.

Above: Virginia Grey was groomed for stardom by MGM, but it never happened. Instead, she became a well-liked and durable supporting actress. This portrait was taken by Laszlo Willinger.

Above left: Cinematographer Harry Stradling Sr is seen here in a posed publicity still which served to advertise MGM's 'endless search' for new talent.

Above right: Clarence Bull's portrait of Lynn Carver gave her the look of a star, but she never became one.

Facing page: Beverly Thompson was a teenage showgirl at Earl Carroll's Nightclub on Sunset Boulevard when Paramount Studios took her on as a starlet. At Paramount, she could no longer be photographed in this fashion! This portrait was taken by Gene Lester.

Above: A more exotic use of Technicolor was seen in Alexander Korda's **The Thief of Bagdad**, a British-American co-production released in 1940 through United Artists. Pictured are Sabu as the Thief and John Justin as the young King Ahmed, in a portrait by John Engstead.

Facing page: The cleverly laconic Gary Cooper entered the 1940s with a Cecil B DeMille Technicolor epic, **The Northwest Mounted Police**, produced at Paramount in 1940. Of course, it was a huge success.

Above: Conrad Veidt gave a memorable performance as the wizard Jaffar. **The Thief Of Bagdad** was begun in England, but the horror of the Blitz chased it to Hollywood where Alexander Korda completed the clever work of Michael Powell and Ludwig Berger. It remains the definitive version of the tale, complete with a beautiful Princess, a mechanical horse and Rex Ingram's scary 'genie in the bottle.'

Pages 54–55: Jaffar and his henchmen enter the palace in order to kidnap the Princess. This is an excerpt from Miles Malleson's screenplay:

> *Jaffar:* I have powers that could force you to my will but I want more than they can give. I want your love. Forget Ahmed. He is no longer blind. For men with eyes, the world is full of women. Only *I* am cursed, because I can see only *you* . . . .

Above: Clark Gable's post-**Gone With The Wind** roles revealed a mastery of comedy that is often obscured by his enduring sex appeal. His deft playing in **Comrade X** was followed by the robust **Boom Town**, again with Hedy Lamarr. Photo left to right: Spencer Tracy, Hedy Lamarr, Claudette Colbert and Clark Gable in Jack Conway's **Boom Town**, a 1940 MGM production.

Facing page: Hedy Lamarr had one of her funniest roles as 'Theodore' in King Vidor's **Comrade X**, thanks to a script by Ben Hecht and Charles Lederer—who had more than a passing acquaintance with the foibles of Communist Russia. The film was a 1940 MGM production. The following is an excerpt from the screenplay.

Mack: American men are usually all alike, all interested in only one thing.
Theo: Money.
Mack: Oh, worse than that...Why, over there men look on women as...as just toys, to have fun with. Nothing more. Not to exchange views on economics with and, uh, things like that.
Theo: That's awful. Makes me feel sad.
Mack: Me too.

Above: Robert Taylor and Vivien Leigh in a Willinger portrait from **Waterloo Bridge**.

Facing Page: James Stewart won an Oscar for his performance in **The Philadelphia Story**. This portrait was done by Clarence Sinclair Bull.

Below: I found this unretouched proof from the celebrated **Waterloo Bridge** sitting in San Francisco's Memory Shop West. Vivien Leigh looks not much different from Laszlo Willinger's finished portraits, nor from her portrayal of the tragic Myra.

Above: Mary Astor and Humphrey Bogart starred in **The Maltese Falcon**, which was produced in 1941 at Warner Brothers. This film was the auspicious debut of director John Huston.

Below: Here is Huston himself, as he and three of his players pose for one of the 'gag' shots that were so popular at the time — they were made as much for mementos as for publicity; these people genuinely enjoyed working together. Photo left to right: Huston, Peter Lorre, Mary Astor and Humphrey Bogart.

Facing page: Cary Grant was charming but troubled in Hitchcock's **Suspicion**.

Pages 62–63: Alan Mowbray and Vivien Leigh in Alexander Korda's 1941 United Artists production, **That Hamilton Woman**. Rene Hubert's gowns, Rudolph Maté's photography and Miss Leigh's performance — not to mention the screenplay by Walter Reisch and RC Sherriff — elevated this film to classic status. Here is an excerpt:

> *Sir William:* Look at this statue. Two hundred years in a Greek temple, then thrown into the mud by some barbarian soldier. Two thousand years sinking lower and lower into the mud, then dug up by the plow of a peasant. Changing hands every year, until at last...it comes to its rightful place...into the hands of someone who understands the glory of its beauty because, my friend, it is still beautiful, isn't it? *Despite* its past....

Above: Clark Gable in Jack Conway's **Honky Tonk**, a 1941 MGM production.

Facing page: Vivien Leigh in a cut scene from **That Hamilton Woman**.

Above: Besides introducing American filmgoers to the basically British **The Thief Of Bagdad** and **That Hamilton Woman**, United Artists brought them two American films with an equally continental flair. Julien Duvivier's **Lydia** starred Merle Oberon as a philanthropic Boston beauty. She is shown here with Alan Marshall in one of the film's distinguished ballroom scenes; costumes were by Walter Plunkett and Marcel Vertes, and photography was by Lee Garmes. The following is an excerpt from the Ben Hecht-Sam Hoffenstein screenplay.

Lydia: Do you remember the ballroom? My breath stopped when I went in...I've seen a great many ballrooms since, very nice ones, but none as wonderful as that one...I entered the room as one enters in a dream, walking on air...do you remember the graceful way people walked on those mirror-like floors? Thousands of mirrors on the walls...the chandeliers hanging from the ceiling like enormous magnolias...do you remember the hundreds of harps? The divine aggregation of musicians, hundreds of them, I think...I often wonder what became of those melting violins...and the wonderful room full of Prince Charmings...do you remember it?

Above: The other United Artists revelation of 1941 was Josef von Sternberg's **The Shanghai Gesture**, which starred Walter Huston, but actually showcased Gene Tierney and Victor Mature, shown here. Most of the film takes place in 'Mother Gin Sling's Casino,' a setting originally conceived in 1927 by playwright John Colton, but not as a casino! From the Geza Herczeg-Jules Furthman screenplay:

Victoria/Poppy: He'll stay *here*. What right have you to command me? I have no more connection with you than with a toad out in the street. 'Mother'...Why don't you forget that litany! Somebody had to be my mother, but I can tell you one thing: if I had my choice, you'd be the last one on earth I'd pick — MOTHER GIN SLING!

Above: Mother Gin Sling presides over the roulette table and over the destinies of her clients. Victoria's initial impression of the casino is expressed in the following excerpt from the screenplay.

Victoria/Poppy: If anyone saw us coming in here, I'd certainly hear plenty. The other places are like kindergartens compared with this. It smells so incredibly evil...I didn't think such a place existed, except in my own imagination...it has a ghastly familiarity, like a half-remembered dream. Anything could happen here...any moment....

Above, left: Gene Tierney, as Victoria Charteris, poses against a mural painted by actor Keye Luke. The addictive pleasures of Mother Gin Sling's milieu drag Victoria from finishing-school propriety to sybaritic dissipation, and she becomes known as 'Poppy,' an uncensorable allusion to her favorite pleasure.

Above right: Ona Munson in the role of Mother Gin Sling, which was originally intended for Marlene Dietrich. In John Colton's scandalous play, the character was named Mother Goddam. According to Los Angeles-based film historian David Chierichetti, Dietrich had agreed to work with Sternberg for the first time in five years, sandwiching **Shanghai Gesture** between Leisen's **The Lady Is Willing** (see page 110) and a commitment to entertain the troops at the front. While making **Lady**, she broke her foot, and the delay in completing that film pushed her schedule past Sternberg's. Then USO work loomed larger than the reunion with her mentor, and they agreed that he should cast someone else in the part. Marlene left for Europe, making headlines because she was wearing pants *and* walking with a cane.

Above: The feisty, multitalented energetic James Cagney—known affectionately in his prime as 'Jimmy'—holds center stage in the 1942 Warner Brothers production of **Yankee Doodle Dandy**. Jimmy won an Oscar for his song-and-dance portrayal of the film's central character, George M Cohan.

Above: James Cagney and his leading lady Joan Leslie (who began her career as Joan Brodel), with extras and a film crew, on the stage set of **Yankee Doodle Dandy**.

Above: Life began anew for Ginger Rogers when she won an Oscar for her performance in Sam Wood's **Kitty Foyle**.

Facing page: Judy Garland left the Andy Hardy series after George B Seitz's **Life Begins For Andy Hardy**, a 1941 MGM production.

Below: Marlene Dietrich was ever mindful of the competition and always aware of camera technique; she'd learned well from Sternberg. In this Mack Elliott photo, she is advising Raoul Walsh on the set of his Warner Brothers film of 1941, **Manpower**.

Above: A portrait of Marlene Dietrich for **Manpower**, probably by Scotty Welbourne.

Facing page: René Clair's **The Flame Of New Orleans**, a 1941 Universal production, was an attempt to transfer Marlene's new-found comic appeal to a more glamorous setting. Marlene was glamorous, of course, but the setting and story were not up to her level.

Above: This William Walling scene still won a Gold Medal for 'Best Posed Production Still' in April 1941, in a competition held by the Academy of Motion Picture Arts and Sciences. The still was shot for **The Flame Of New Orleans**.

Facing page: Upon his arrival in America, Alfred Hitchcock transformed Joan Fontaine from the gushy ingenue of **The Women** to the icy blonde heroine of **Rebecca**, and **Suspicion** *(right)*. He would perform similar casting rituals with other female stars until his last film in 1976.

Facing page: Veronica Lake was blonder and icier, but she warmed the hearts of Paramount executives in successful films like Mitchell Leisen's **I Wanted Wings**. This portrait was made by Eugene Robert Richee in connection with that 1941 film.

Above: The publicity department, curious to see what else could be done with their new sensation, sent Miss Lake over to George Hurrell's gallery, with the results seen here.

Above: Samuel Goldwyn transferred Tallulah Bankhead's stage success to the screen and Bette Davis now 'became' Regina Giddens in William Wyler's **The Little Foxes**, produced in 1941.

Facing page: Another Hurrell portrait of Veronica Lake after **I Wanted Wings**.

Above: The prolific WS Van Dyke II directed **The Thin Man** and **Tarzan**, Crawford and MacDonald-Eddy vehicles, bringing a vibrant energy to all of them. This candid still shows him at work on the set of **The Shadow Of The Thin Man**, produced at MGM in 1941.

Facing page: Lillian Hellman provided as evil a character for Bette in **The Little Foxes** as had Somerset Maugham in previous years; Miss Hellman also worked on the screenplay, along with Dorothy Parker and Alan Campbell, among others.

Pages 82–83: Van Dyke's version of Noel Coward's **Bittersweet** provided portraitist Clarence Bull with an opportunity to photograph the most popular singing team of the era, Jeanette MacDonald and Nelson Eddy.

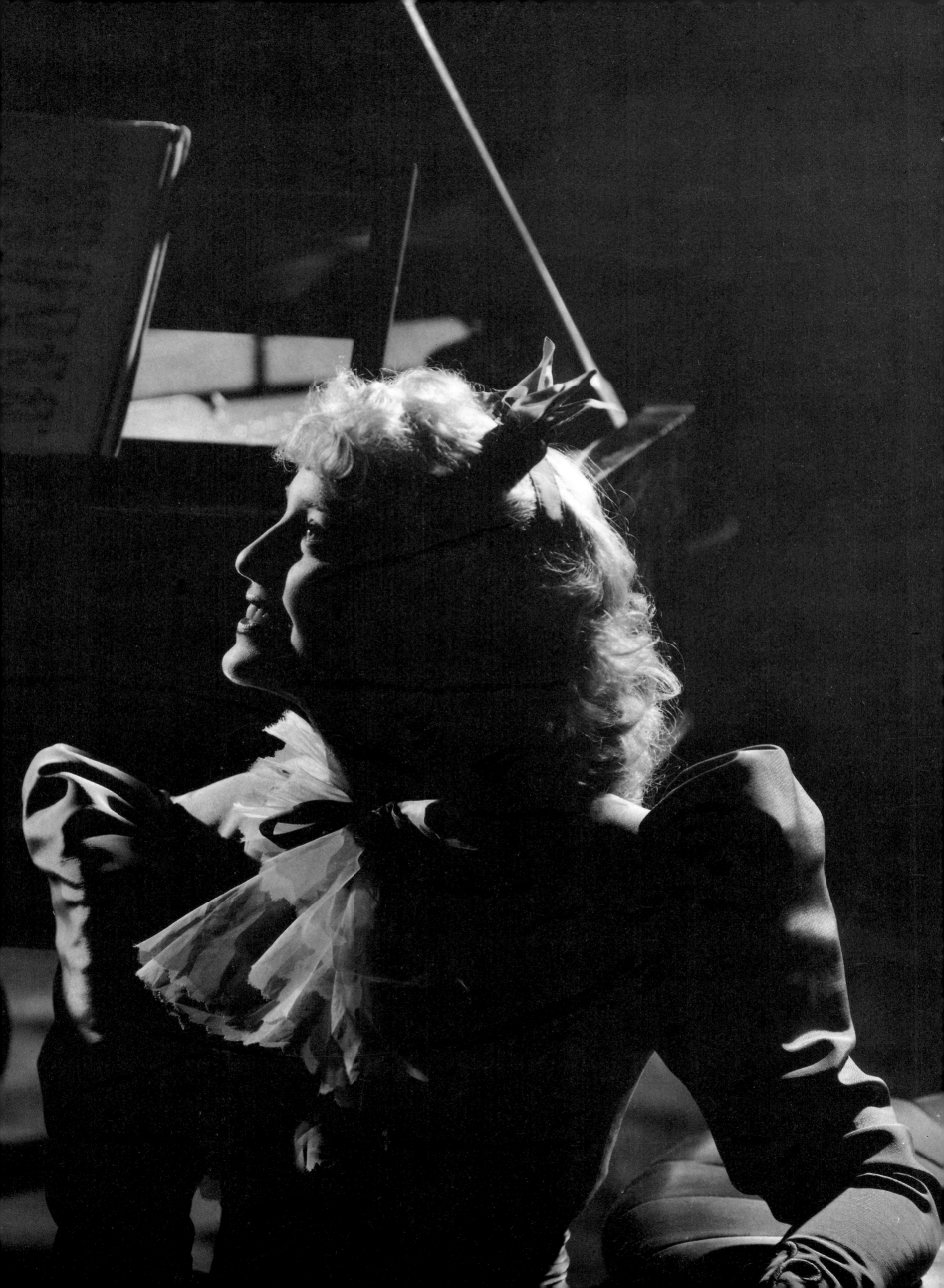

Above: Joan Crawford (seen here with Conrad Veidt and Melvyn Douglas) once again benefited from patient and inventive direction in George Cukor's **A Woman's Face**—produced at MGM in 1941—and from a script by Elliot Paul and the clever Donald Ogden Stewart. The following is an excerpt.

Ingrid: The 'wonder girl' has also tried poetry, painting—and alcohol.

Facing page: Joan Crawford went to George Hurrell's portrait gallery for a sitting in connection with **A Woman's Face**.

Pages 86–87: Irving Rapper's **Now Voyager**, a 1942 Warner Brothers production, made real the dream of an ugly duckling turned globe-trotting swan. Here we see Paul Henreid and Bette Davis in a sound stage re-creation of Rio de Janeiro, and the following is from the touching Casey Robinson script:

Jerry: Do you believe in immortality?

Charlotte: I don't know. Do you?

Jerry: I want to believe that there's a chance for such happiness to be . . . carried on, somehow, somewhere . . . .

Charlotte: Are you so happy, then?

Jerry: Close to it. And getting 'warmer and warmer,' as we used to say as kids. Remember?

Charlotte: 'Look out or you'll get burned,' we used to say . . . no, I'm immune to happiness and therefore to burns.

Above: Bette Davis' characterization of Charlotte Vale in **Now Voyager** remains one of her finest achievements.

Facing page: World War II propaganda can only partially be blamed for the misfire that was John Huston's 1942 Warner Brothers production, **Across The Pacific**. Not even the star power of Mary Astor and Humphrey Bogart could save the film that John Huston deserted—to go to war to make *real* propaganda films.

Pages 90–91: Joseph Ruttenberg's cinematography made this indoor setting 'feel' right in Mervyn LeRoy's **Random Harvest**, which starred Greer Garson and Ronald Colman.

Above left: Spencer Tracy and Hedy Lamarr enacted John Stein-beck's timeless tale in Victor Fleming's **Tortilla Flat**, which was produced in 1942 at MGM.

Above right: Richard Carlson was enslaved by Hedy Lamarr's Tondelayo, '...that chocolate Cleopatra,' in Richard Thorpe's **White Cargo**, another MGM production of 1942.

Facing page: Hedy Lamarr's portrayal of Tondelayo was in a category of its own—how many Africans have Viennese accents? —but the film was beautifully photographed by Harry Stradling and the script was wonderfully overwritten. Here is an excerpt from Leon Gordon's adaptation of his own 1920 play:

   Doctor: Of course, you do know just who and...what she is. She knows how to purr her way into your mind...and scratch her way out. Always taking and never giving...
   Lanford: She's the nearest thing to a civilized woman I've seen in five impossible months....

Below: Clarence Bull's camera catches Hedy Lamarr 'relaxing' at home, and finally we get to see her own shade of makeup.

Above: Produced in 1941 at MGM, Ingrid Bergman's third American film was WS Van Dyke's **A Rage In Heaven**.

Facing page: A suddenly matured Judy Garland was now on the scene, making films like Busby Berkeley's 1942 MGM production of **For Me And My Gal**.

Above: Cast at her own insistence as Ivy Pearson in Victor Fleming's 1942 MGM production of **Dr Jekyll and Mr Hyde**, Ingrid Bergman made critics and audiences alike take notice—not to mention the surviving superstars at MGM. MacDonald, Loy, Shearer, Crawford and Garbo were all aware of the buildup being given to Bergman, Garland, Lamarr, Garson and Turner...and what it signified for themselves.

The 1940s brought what I refer to as the 'Twilight of the Goddesses.' The leading ladies who had filled America's dreams (and MGM's coffers) since 1925 now decided — one by one — that what becomes a legend *most* is . . . a graceful exit.

Above: When each exit finally occurred, it was as noteworthy as any Adrian-gowned entrance had ever been. Jeanette MacDonald ended the operetta series with WS Van Dyke's **I Married An Angel**, produced in 1942. She is seen here conferring with 'Woody,' with whom she would make her last MGM film as a star.

Facing page: **Cairo** was Jeanette MacDonald's swan song; Woody Van Dyke passed away less than a year later.

Above: When Myrna Loy finished Van Dyke's **Shadow Of The Thin Man** and then left MGM, Norma Shearer—the formidable First Lady of that formidable studio—took stock of her options, made two more films, and did the same.

Miss Shearer's penultimate offering was RZ Leonard's **We Were Dancing**, a 1942 production—and it was as silly as this portrait.

Facing page: Norma Shearer's last film was George Cukor's **Her Cardboard Lover**, which was produced in 1942. Shearer had the accumulated skill and elegance of her nearly 20 years of stardom, Cukor's direction and the excellent support of Bob Taylor and George Sanders. She even had the advantage of a witty stage play adapted by the playwright; unfortunately, she had the insurmountable disadvantage of a tacked-on third act and its attendant slapstick. The resulting film was not up to the brilliant opening scene, from which the following is an excerpt.

Consuelo Croydon: You've been following me for several days now. Let me tell you: making a doormat of yourself never gets you anywhere. A man—or a woman—in love who clings, begs, follows...how little hope there is in it...and how much pain. You're a man. Stand on your own feet. Have strength, restraint...and a little pride!

Joan Crawford's decision to 'leave Metro' was not forced on her by Louis B Mayer, but was the result of a long period of deliberation. Her dramatic talents had been ill-served by a series of unworthy films, the last of which was Richard Thorpe's 1943 film **Above Suspicion**, in which she co-starred with Fred MacMurray and Conrad Veidt (pictured *above*). This film may or may not have helped the war effort, but it was not the showcase Joan needed. To quote from the script by Keith Winter, Melville Baker and Patricia Coleman: 'A rose by any other name—stinks!'

Facing page: The most deliberate goddess of all made the most decisive exit, and this film was the cause. Turn the page to see...

Facing page: Constance Bennett and Greta Garbo in a powder room scene from George Cukor's **Two-Faced Woman**, produced in 1941.

Greta Garbo decided to call it quits after the film was condemned by the Legion of Decency and ignored by the public. Her contract was '...terminated by mutual agreement.' **Two-Faced Woman**, like Shearer's swan song **Her Cardboard Lover**, suffered from excessive tampering with its essentially clever premise, and from a tacked-on, slapsticky denouement. To see Garbo's sublime talent mired in such ineptitude was more than most could bear; the film was a huge flop.

Above: The few really funny scenes in **Two-Faced Woman** had Constance Bennett and Melvyn Douglas mildly scandalized by Garbo's risqué philosophy. The following is from the screenplay by SN Behrman, Salka Viertel and George Oppenheimer:

Miss Borg: Next to love, everything else is a waste of time. I like *men.* Preferably rich men.

Above: **Two-Faced Woman** underwent considerable rewrites and retakes, as is indicated by this scene — which appears nowhere in the finished film. Ruth Gordon is at photo left.

Above: Another haunting image from the fall of 1941 and yet another talent spurned by Hollywood—if not by fame: Orson Welles as Charles Foster Kane.

Facing page: Clarence Bull made this bittersweet portrait of Greta Garbo, his favorite subject, on 3 October 1941. It was the last time he ever photographed her; the goddesses had all gone now....

Above: In the room that was almost a double for Marion Davies' room in the Hearst Castle, Orson Welles and Dorothy Comingore act out a scene that never really happened between William Randolph Hearst and Marion Davies; all the more reason for Hearst to marshal the harpies of Hollywood against Welles. An excerpt from the screenplay:

Kane: Susan...please don't go. No. Please, Susan. From now on, everything will be exactly the way you want it to be, not the way I think you want it, but...your way. Hm? You mustn't go...you can't do this to me....

Susan: I see...it's *you* that this is being done to. It's not me at all. It's not what it means to *me*. I can't do this to you? Oh, yes, I *can*.

Facing page: 'I don't know how to run a newspaper. I just try everything I can,' says Charlie Kane, and we wonder if that was one of the speeches Orson Welles wrote in his collaboration with Herman Mankiewicz and John Houseman. Welles, a mere 25 years old, had also assumed the task of producing and directing this, his first film.

Above: Welles directs and acts in the scene in which he gets out the first edition of Kane's newly acquired *Inquirer*.

Below: Welles is obviously in character as he rehearses Kane's embarrassing applause for Susan; dress extras behind him are relaxing, unaware of the impact this film will have.

Above: Welles' next film was butchered by studio executives, but the remains are still fascinating; shown here is Agnes Moorehead in **The Magnificent Ambersons**, produced in 1942 at RKO.

Below: His third completed film fared slightly better; here, we see Dolores Del Rio in **Journey Into Fear**, a 1943 RKO production.

Above: **The Lady Is Willing**, produced in 1942 by Columbia, was a confectionery offering by Mitchell Leisen that put Marlene Dietrich in a Latin American musical number entitled 'I Find Love.' Behind those bugle beads, her foot was probably in a cast!

Below: Busby Berkeley's 1943 Fox production, **The Gang's All Here** also reflected that era's interest in exotic rhythms — especially as performed by the inimitable Carmen Miranda, here singing 'The Lady In The Tutti Frutti Hat,' before the onslaught of dozens of giant Technicolor bananas.

Above: Teresa Wright co-starred with Gary Cooper in Sam Wood's
The Pride Of The Yankees. George Hurrell made this 1942
portrait for the Goldwyn Studios publicity department.

Above: Alan Ladd became a star in Frank Tuttle's 1942 Paramount production of **This Gun For Hire**.

Facing page: A portrait of Claude Rains by Ray Jones; the horror genre was on its last legs when Universal injected it with Technicolor *and* Nelson Eddy in an attempt to revive it. The revival was short-lived, and Arthur Lubin's **The Phantom Of The Opera** survives as one of the more awkward examples of mixing the genres of horror and operetta. By 1943, horror films were giving way to a new genre.

Below: Errol Flynn sustained his popularity by alternating between period and modern roles, and by keeping his off-screen image equally energetic.

The new genre had no name at the time, but it has since earned the descriptive title *film noir*. One of its first practitioners was Val Lewton, of **Cat People** fame. A lesser-known but equally eerie film produced by him is Mark Robson's **The Seventh Victim**, released in 1943 by RKO, which featured Jean Brooks (*above*) as a repentant devil-worshipper who inadvertently drags her innocent sister into a cauldron of intrigue.

Facing page: The strange lifestyle of Jean Brooks' character was symbolized by the use of part of Jonne Donne's 'Holy Sonnet I' in the opening and closing scenes of the film:

I runne to death, and death meets me as fast,
and all my pleasures are like yesterday.

Above: Humphrey Bogart and Ingrid Bergman starred in Michael Curtiz's **Casablanca**, a 1943 Warner Brothers film that affects each viewer as only a great work of art can: the time and place of its first viewing is indelibly etched in memory. In my case, it was a Saturday night full-house screening in USC's huge Bovard Auditorium. I was in the second row. In the first was the evening's guest of honor, Jack L Warner, making what was probably his last public appearance. The date was 1 December 1973.

Facing page: Fifty-four-year-old Claude Rains earned $4000 a week for his portrayal of Louis Renault in **Casablanca**, which is a paltry sum when compared to the rich legacy of character work he left film audiences.

Above: Ingrid Bergman as Ilsa Laszlo, in a scene still from the flashback sequence. Evident here is the subtle yet evocative mood of this great motion picture. 'Play it again, Sam,' one of the most misquoted dramatic lines ever spoken, even now remains part of the national—and international—consciousness. What Bogart actually said was, 'You played it for her. Now play it for me. Play it, Sam.'

Facing page: Another glimpse of the leading lady of the archetypal wartime love story. It seems strange that, at one point, two resolutions were mapped out for **Casablanca**—but when the fog-shrouded parting at the runway was filmed, it was immediately apparent that this film could not have any other ending.

Facing page: Hedy Lamarr as seen by Laszlo Willinger in a portrait made to exploit Alexander Hall's 1943 MGM production of **Heavenly Body**. The costume unfortunately does not appear in the film.

Above: Vincent Sherman's **Old Acquaintance**, a 1943 Warner Brothers production, gave Bette Davis and Miriam Hopkins the occasion to do what Shearer and Crawford never could...

...but certainly wanted to. The candid camera caught this moment (*below*), and if the hostility looks real, that's because it was!

Above: A Clarence Bull portrait of Judy Garland from 1943.

Facing page: Miss Garland starred in Norman Taurog's **Presenting Lily Mars**, produced by MGM in 1943. This portrait was made by Eric Carpenter.

Above: Bette Davis had a showy, multi-costume role in Vincent Sherman's 1944 Warner Brothers production, **Mr Skeffington.**

Facing page: Gary Cooper, circa 1944.

Above: Claire Trevor and Dick Powell square off in **Murder, My Sweet**—John Paxton's adaptation of Raymond Chandler's *Farewell, My Lovely*, and Chandler's favorite film of his work.

Facing page: Claire Trevor as Mrs Grayle in Edward Dmytryk's **Murder, My Sweet**, produced in 1944 at RKO.

Above: Having missed the opportunity to play Mother Gin Sling, Marlene Dietrich made up for it by playing an Arabian enchantress in William Dieterle's **Kismet**, a 1944 MGM production.

Facing page: Wealthy Mrs Grayle is revealed as Velma Valento, a double-dealing murderess, in the climax of **Murder, My Sweet**. Her classic line: 'You know, this will be the first time I've ever killed anyone I knew so little and liked so well.'

Above: Margaret O'Brien and Judy Garland shone with a nostalgic glow in Vincente Minnelli's nostalgic **Meet Me In St Louis**, an MGM production of 1944.

Facing page: This mirrored portrait of Lucille Ball was made in connection with the 1944 MGM production of **Meet The People** by Laszlo Willinger.

Above: Championed initially by Rudy Vallee, Alice Faye was queen of the Fox musicals in the latter 1930s and early 1940s. When Betty Grable became her rival at Fox, Alice's star began its decline.

Above: Betty Grable was *the* pinup 'girl next door.' American servicemen fought World War II to make the world safe for girls like Betty.

Above: Bogart and Bacall in the restaurant scene from Warner Brothers' 1946 release **The Big Sleep**. Bogart turned in an admirably tough performance as Raymond Chandler's hardboiled detective, Philip Marlowe, and Bacall was quite equal to the role of being his leading lady.

Facing page: Humphrey Bogart sported a new co-star, 19 year old ex-model Lauren Bacall, in Howard Hawks' **To Have and Have Not**, produced at Warner Brothers in 1945.

Above: The traumatic interrogation that formed the innermost flashback of John Brahm's **The Locket**, a 1946 RKO film, was scripted so skillfully by Sheridan Gibney that it's difficult to decide if Nancy Monks (Sharyn Moffett) is really guilty or if Mrs Willis (Katherine Emery) is needlessly harsh. An excerpt from the screenplay:

Mrs Willis: Nancy, I need your assistance. The little locket... has disappeared. I'm not making any charges, mind you. I merely want you to help the servants look for it. And if you should find it, I'll give you something very nice as a reward.

Nancy: I didn't take it, Mrs Willis. I don't see why you blame me.

Mrs Willis: I'm not blaming you, Nancy. I haven't said I thought anyone took it.

Nancy: Then why do you talk to me like this?

Mrs Willis: Because the thought did occur to me that sometimes little girls have a way of finding things.

Nancy: I'm not a little girl... I know what stealing is!

Mrs Willis: I did not use the word 'steal.'

Nancy: You meant it, though!

Mrs Willis: I meant nothing of the sort. Children take things, to be sure. I don't consider that stealing. Much worse than taking things is to lie about it.

Nancy: I'm not lying! I haven't got it and I don't know where it is!

Above: Nancy Monks (Laraine Day) has grown up and her childhood trauma comes back to haunt her upon encountering her future mother-in-law, none other than Mrs Willis (Katherine Emery). So begins the nightmarish climax of **The Locket**, which was originally entitled **What Nancy Wanted**, because of the admonition given early in the film by Nancy's mother (Helen Thimig): 'It's all right to want things, Nancy, but you'll have to be patient. If you want things badly enough, someday you'll have them . . .'

Below: Van Heflin came back to town in order to undo a childhood wrong perpetrated by Barbara Stanwyck, in Lewis Milestone's 1946 Paramount production, **The Strange Love Of Martha Ivers**.

Above: No one expected Tay Garnett to make a bad girl of Lana Turner, but he certainly did in his 1946 MGM masterpiece **The Postman Always Rings Twice**.

Facing page: MGM manufactured Ava Gardner from a Southern girl whose portrait a talent scout had seen in a photographer's window. She was much better photographed at MGM — especially by Clarence Bull, who made this portrait.

Pages 140–141: John Garfield and Lana Turner generate sexual tension in this scene from **The Postman Always Rings Twice**.

Above: Lana Turner makes a historic entrance in **The Postman Always Rings Twice**.

Facing page: This is Jennifer Jones in character as Pearl Chavez, 'a tempestuous half-breed' in King Vidor's **Duel in the Sun**, a 1946 Selznick production. Pearl Chavez was portrayed as a 'wildflower, sprung from the hard clay...quick to blossom...and early to die....' Her badness was represented as having been inherited from her Indian mother, who was portrayed by the legendary Tilly Losch.

Above: King Vidor's Technicolor epic opens with a scene that he
didn't direct. Producer Selznick, indulging his penchant for rewrit-
ing, firing and re-shooting, had William Dieterle direct a new
opening sequence. It featured a writhing dance choreographed and
performed by Tilly Losch, essaying the part of a wanton exhibition-
ist. She performed the dance to sensational music by Dmitri
Tiomkin, twitching to Indian drums while splashed with light from
red and amber gels.

Facing page: Painter, writer, choreographer and dancer — Austrian
Tilly Losch, for once in repose.

Above: Ava Gardner acquired her 'bad girl' training while on loan from MGM—to studios like Universal for films like Robert Siodmak's **The Killers**, which was made in 1946.

Facing page: After 11 years of trial and error, Rita Hayworth found her role—Charles Vidor's **Gilda**, a 1946 Columbia production.

Above left: In 1946, Jennifer Jones was but one of many post-war femmes fatales.

Above right: David O Selznick hired Josef von Sternberg to give Jennifer Jones his magic touch—and indeed, through much of the film Pearl Chavez has that Paramount glow of the 1930s.

Above: In Edmund Goulding's **The Razor's Edge**, a 1946 Fox production, Somerset Maugham (Herbert Marshall) shifts the literary focus from his protagonist Tyrone Power (not pictured) to...

...Gene Tierney (*below*) in the role which was her least sympathetic, but most watchable.

Facing page: The icy tigress of **The Razor's Edge**. This speech by Lamar Trotti gives her rationalization for breaking up Tyrone Power's romance with Anne Baxter:

> *Isabel:* I know women. Do you think she'll stick to Larry? Of course not. Sooner or later she'll break out. It's in her blood. It's the brute she wants. That's what excites her. It's a brute she'll go after. She'll lead Larry to hell!

Pages 150–151: Gene Tierney redeemed herself by playing a gentle romantic in Joseph L Mankiewicz's 1947 Fox production of **The Ghost And Mrs Muir**.

Facing page: Michael Redgrave menaces Joan Bennett in Fritz Lang's **The Secret Beyond The Door**, a 1947 Universal *film noir* in which, for once, the villain was not a woman.

Above: Another superb cad was George Sanders' eponymous character in Albert Lewin's **The Private Affairs Of Bel Ami**, a 1947 United Artists film which was notable for Gordon Wiles' art direction and for the understated performances of Ann Dvorak, Angela Lansbury and Katherine Emery.

Below: Hurd Hatfield and Audrey Totter sit at Claude Rains' well-stocked bar in Michael Curtiz's **The Unsuspected**, a 1947 Warner Brothers production.

Above: The 'baddest' bad girl of the *film noir* era must surely be Jane Greer. In Jacques Tourneur's **Out Of The Past**, a 1947 RKO production, she plays Cathy Moffet, a slinky enigma who lives only to cross and double-cross.

Facing page: **Out Of The Past** is considered by many to be the finest *film noir* ever made. Director Tourneur admonished actress Greer: 'Be impassive.' As she cuts a swath of evil through the film, she is nothing *but* impassive, even when confronted by an angry Kirk Douglas.

Pages 156–157: Nicholas Musuraca's low-key photography set the mood for the scene in which the black widow ensnares her latest victim.

Above: Cathy Moffett decides the outcome of a fight.

Facing page: The quintessential *film noir* image—an evil woman awakened from guilty dreams.

Above: What begins for Robert Mitchum in an Acapulco bar...
ends with a death sentence from Cathy Moffett. But then, the film
was based on a novel entitled *Build My Gallows High*, by Daniel
Mainwaring, who also scripted the film. An excerpt:

Cathy: Remember the mountains...higher than these, and
always snow on them? We should have stayed there.

Jeff: I'm trying to remember something else.

Cathy: I never told you I was anything but what I am. You just
wanted to imagine I was. That's why I left you. Now we're back
to stay. We're starting all over. I want to go back to Mexico. I
want to walk out of the sun again and find you waiting. I want to
sit in the same moonlight and tell you all the things I never told
you, until you don't hate me, until sometime you love again.

Facing page: In 1947, Humphrey Bogart earned $467,000.

Above: In the postwar years, Marlene Dietrich returned to Paramount, where she continued to administer, define and personify glamour. Here she is in a scene from Billy Wilder's 1948 film, **A Foreign Affair**.

Facing page: Joan Crawford saved her career by changing studios, winning an Oscar, and then avoiding the clichéd roles that had plagued her at MGM. This portrait was made to publicize Jean Negulesco's **Humoresque**, a 1947 Warner Brothers production which contains what may be Crawford's most telling performance.

Above and facing page: Dietrich's portrait sitting for Mitchell Leisen's **Golden Earrings**, made in 1947.

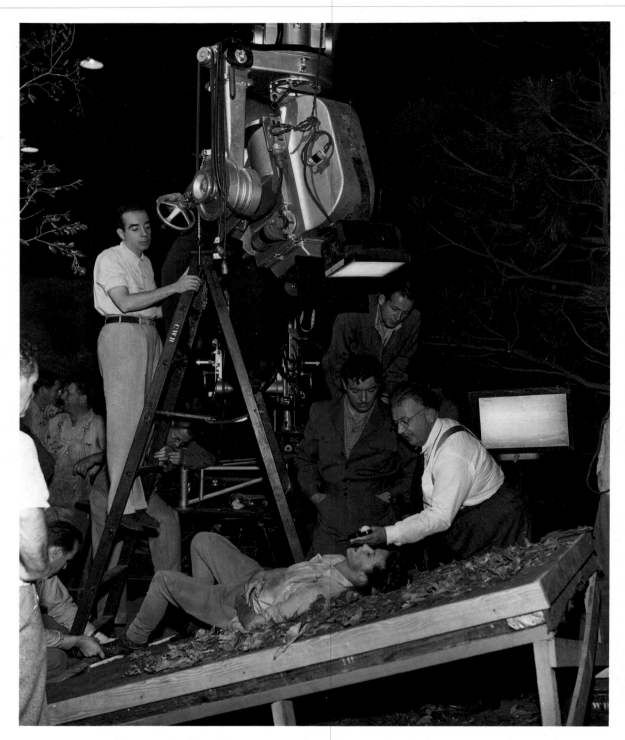

Above: As the 1940s drew to a close, and television became a reality, the studios tried new variations on old themes — usually with old faces. Robert Taylor returned from World War II and felt fortunate to be cast opposite Katharine Hepburn, albeit playing a now-fashionable psychopath. The film was Vincente Minnelli's **Undercurrent**, a 1946 MGM production. This production still shows Minnelli (on ladder), and Taylor standing over Hepburn, while the co-inventor of the light meter, Karl Freund, utilizes his 11-year old invention.

Facing page: Hedy Lamarr floated from studio to studio in the late 1940s, finally financing her own productions, including this one, **The Strange Woman**.

Above: Lauren Bacall and Humphrey Bogart co-starred for the fourth and last time in John Huston's 1948 Warner Brothers production, **Key Largo**.

Facing page: Maureen O'Hara's coloring was ideally suited to the Technicolor epics in which she so often appeared.

Pages 170–171: Ava Gardner and musicians in veteran director Robert Z Leonard's **The Bribe**, a 1948 MGM production.

Pages 172–173: Stealing the show in both **The Bribe** and John Farrow's **The Big Clock** was the one and only Charles Laughton — here menacing Rita Johnson.

Above: Barbara Stanwyck gave the performance of a lifetime in Anatole Litvak's **Sorry, Wrong Number**, a 1948 Paramount production.

Facing page: Here are Miss Stanwyck and an up-and-coming actor named Burt Lancaster, who played her husband in **Sorry, Wrong Number**.

Above: An expensive production that was shot on location, and then re-shot in the studio (thanks to compulsive tampering by David Selznick), was William Dieterle's **Portrait Of Jennie**, a 1949 Selznick production.

Above: The inspired cinematography credited to Joseph August was actually the work of Lee Garmes, who stepped in to finish (and eventually re-shoot most of) the production when August died suddenly. The following is an excerpt from Ben Hecht's screenplay.

Jennie: Eben, do you think people can know what lies ahead? I mean, what's going to happen to them? You know how you feel sad about things sometimes? About things that have never happened...perhaps they're the things that are going to happen to us...perhaps we know it, and we're just afraid to admit it to ourselves....

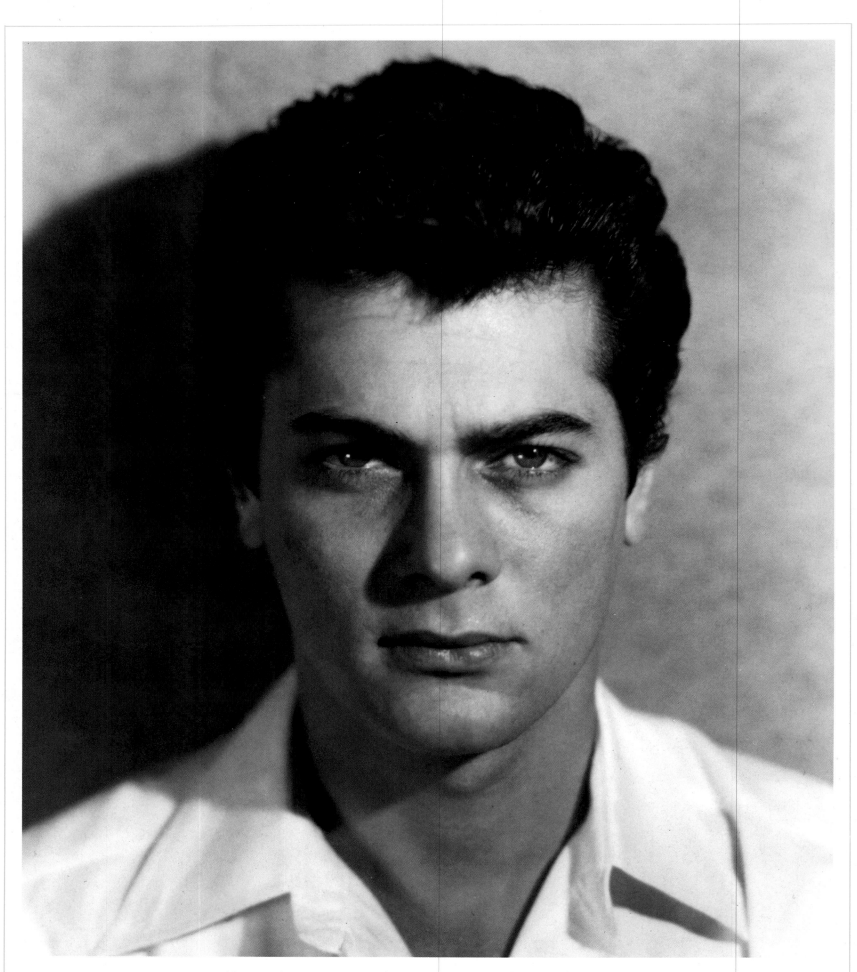

Above: The post-war studios were constantly on the lookout for new talent, vying as they were with television. This young man from Brooklyn was a 1950 discovery; his name was changed from Bernie Schwartz to Tony Curtis.

Facing page: Alan Ladd's career began to falter in the late 1940s despite attempts to broaden his range with offbeat roles like **The Great Gatsby**. His bread and butter, though, was paid for by continuing to appear in 'actioners' like **Saigon**.

Above: The year 1950 was distinguished by two peerless performances. The first was delivered by Bette Davis in Joseph L Mankiewicz's Fox production, **All About Eve**.

Facing page: The second was delivered by Gloria Swanson in Billy
Wilder's **Sunset Boulevard**, which was produced at Paramount.

Above: An informal group shot on the set of Sunset Boulevard's strangest residence: Buster Keaton, HB Warner, Anna Q Nilsson, Erich von Stroheim, Gloria Swanson and William Holden. This was a great moment in Swanson's career, and a happy project for all involved.

Facing page: The still camera caught the fury of Gloria Swanson's Norma Desmond as she hit an ungrateful Joe Gillis on New Year's Eve. Gloria had gotten the part when Billy Wilder was turned down by his original choice, Mary Pickford.

Above: The 1950s had an atmosphere that was not conducive to genuine *film noir*. What emerged were strange combinations of suspense and comedy, like John Farrow's (nonetheless entertaining) **His Kind Of Woman**, an RKO production of 1951. Shown here are Leslye Banning, Robert Mitchum and Charles McGraw in an atmospheric setup lit by Jack Wild.

Facing page: **His Kind Of Woman** was a Howard Hughes production and Jane Russell was indeed what the title stated, so she performed her obligatory songs, including the irritatingly catchy 'Five Little Miles From San Berdoo,' by Paramount veteran San Coslow. To borrow a line from the Frank Fenton-Jack Leonard script, 'It had a message no pigeon would carry.'

years apart in Charles Walters' 1949 MGM production **The Barkleys of Broadway**. This unexpected treat for their fans occurred because of a last-minute casting switch: Ginger Rogers replaced an ailing Judy Garland, thus bolstering her own career.

Facing page: Most accounts portray Astaire and Rogers as consummate professionals whose only disagreements were over fine points of the complex art of screen dancing.

Index

Astaire, Fred: 16, 17, 42, 186, 187
Astor, Mary: 18, 61, 89

Bacall, Lauren: 134, 135, 168
Ball, Lucille: 131
Banning, Leslye: 184
Bennett, Constance: 102, 103
Bennett, Joan: 152
Bergman, Ingrid: 95, 117, 118, 119
Bogart, Humphrey: 18, 28, 61, 89, 117, 134, 135, 161, 167
Boland, Mary: 10, 12
Bolger, Ray: 8–9, 24
Brando, Marlon: 188
Brooks, Jean: 114, 115

Cagney, James: 68, 69, 178, 179
Carlson, Richard: 92
Carver, Lynn: 50
Colbert, Claudette: 57
Colman, Ronald: 90–91
Comingore, Dorothy: 106
Cooper, Gary: 52, 111, 125
Cotten, Joseph: 176
Crawford, Joan: 10, 11, 12, 14–15, 42, 43, 49, 84, 85, 100, 162
Cukor, George: 10, 12
Curtis, Tony: 178

Davis, Bette: 33, 38–39, 40, 41, 79, 80, 86–87, 88, 121, 124, 180
de Havilland, Olivia: 22
Del Rio, Dolores: 109
Dietrich, Marlene: 7, 34, 42, 71–74, 110, 129, 163–165, 192
Douglas, Kirk: 155, 156–157
Douglas, Melvyn: 84, 103

Eddy, Nelson: 48, 82–83
Emery, Katherine: 136

Faye, Alice: 132
Flynn, Errol: 29, 112
Fontaine, Joan: 4–5, 10, 75
Freund, Karl: 166

Gable, Clark: 20, 21, 22, 43, 57, 64
Garbo, Greta: 24, 101–104
Gardner, Ava: 2–3, 138, 147, 170–171
Garfield, John: 140–141
Garland, Judy: 8–9, 24, 35, 70, 94, 122, 123, 130
Garson, Greer: 90–91
Gillis, Joe: 183
Goddard, Paulette: 10, 12
Gordon, Ruth: 103
Grable, Betty: 133
Grant, Cary: 1, 4–5, 60
Greenstreet, Sydney: 18
Greer, Jane: 154, 155, 156–157
Grey, Virginia: 50

Haley, Jack: 8–9, 24
Hatfield, Hurd: 153
Hayward, Susan: 36
Hayworth, Rita: 16, 146
Heflin, Van: 137
Henreid, Paul: 86–87
Hepburn, Katharine: 42, 45, 46–47, 166
Holden, William: 182
Hopkins, Miriam: 33, 121
Howard, Leslie: 22
Huston, John: 61

Johnson, Rita: 172–173
Jones, Jennifer: 143, 147, 176, 177

Justin, John: 53

Keaton, Buster: 182

Ladd, Alan: 112, 179
Lahr, Bert: 24
Lake, Veronica: 76, 77, 78
Lamarr, Hedy: 56, 57, 92, 93, 120, 167
Lancaster, Burt: 175
Laughton, Charles: 26, 172–173
Leigh, Vivien: 20, 22, 23, 33, 58, 62–63, 65, 188
Leslie, Joan: 69
Lombard, Carole: 30, 31, 32
Lorre, Peter: 18, 19, 61
Losch, Tilly: 144, 145
Lugosi, Bela: 24

MacDonald, Jeanette: 48, 82–83, 96, 97
MacMurray, Fred: 100
March, Fredric: 37, 49
Marshall, Alan: 66
Marshall, Herbert: 148
Mature, Victor: 66, 67
McGraw, Charles: 184
Minnelli, Vincente: 166
Miranda, Carmen: 110
Mitchum, Robert: 160, 184
Moffett, Cathy: 158, 159, 160
Moffett, Sharyn: 136
Moorehead, Agnes: 109
Mowbray, Alan: 62–63
Munson, Ona: 67

Nash, Florence: 10, 12
Nilsson, Anna Q: 182

Oberon, Merle: 66
O'Brien, Margaret: 130
O'Hara, Maureen: 169

Povah, Phyllis: 10, 12
Powell, Dick: 127

Rains, Claude: 113, 116
Redgrave, Michael: 152
Rogers, Ginger: 17, 71, 186, 187
Russell, Jane: 185
Russell, Rosalind: 10, 12, 13, 14–15

Sabu: 53
Sanders, George: 153
Shearer, Norma: 10–12, 14–15, 44, 98, 99
Stanwyck, Barbara: 137, 174, 175
Stewart, James: 59
Stradling, Harry Sr: 50
Stromberg, Hunt: 10
Swanson, Gloria: 181, 182, 183, 190–191

Taylor, Robert: 58, 166
Thompson, Beverly: 51
Tierney, Gene: 66, 67, 137, 148, 150–151
Totter, Audrey: 153
Tracy, Spencer: 46–47, 57, 92
Trevor, Claire: 27, 126, 127, 128
Trotti, Lamar: 149
Turner, Lana: 139, 140–141, 142

Van Dyke, WS II: 81
Veidt, Conrad: 44, 53, 54–55, 84, 100
Von Stroheim, Erich: 182

Walsh, Raoul: 71
Warner, HB: 182
Wayne, John: 27
Welles, Orson: 105–108
Wright, Teresa: 111

Facing page: Madness of a different flavor permeated the screen adaptation of Tennesse Williams' hit play *A Streetcar Named Desire*, and as with **White Heat**, audiences saw aspects of human behavior previously denied them by Hollywood studios. This seldom-seen shot from the Elia Kazan production depicts the pivotal scene in which Stanley Kowalski (Marlon Brando) attacks Blanche DuBois (Vivien Leigh).

Pages 190-191: A movie projector beam becomes a spotlight... the perfect analogy for a film buff's look at images of Hollywood past... Gloria Swanson is gilded by incandescent light—and the tour ends.

Page 192: A portrait of Marlene Dietrich for the 1941 Warner Brothers film, **Manpower** (see also page 71). The gown is by Milo Anderson.